Dearest Arnold,

*The bond between mother and son
is a special one.
It remains unchanged by time or distance....
It is a gift held in the heart and in the soul.*

— Stephanie Douglass

*Love,
mom*

The Bond Between a

Mother & Son

Lasts Forever

A Blue Mountain Arts® Collection
on the Love, Hopes, and Dreams
That Mothers and Sons Share

Edited by Patricia Wayant

Blue Mountain Press™
Boulder, Colorado

We wish to thank Susan Polis Schutz for permission to reprint the following poem that appears in this publication: "To My Son, with Love." Copyright © 1989 by Stephen Schutz and Susan Polis Schutz. All rights reserved.

Library of Congress Control Number: 2003106053
ISBN: 0-88396-765-0 (trade paper) — ISBN: 0-88396-735-9 (hardcover)

ACKNOWLEDGMENTS appear on page 64.

Certain trademarks are used under license.

Manufactured in the United States of America.

 This book is printed on recycled paper.

This book is printed on fine quality, laid embossed, 80 lb. paper. This paper has been specially produced to be acid free (neutral pH) and contains no groundwood or unbleached pulp. It conforms with all the requirements of the American National Standards Institute, Inc., so as to ensure that this book will last and be enjoyed by future generations.

Blue Mountain Arts, Inc.
P.O. Box 4549, Boulder, Colorado 80306

Contents

The Bond Between Mother and Son Lasts a Lifetime

The bond between mother and son is a special one.
It remains unchanged by time or distance.
It is the purest love — unconditional and true.
It is understanding of any situation
and forgiving of any mistake.
It creates a support that is constant
while everything else changes.
It is a friendship based on mutual love, respect,
and a genuine liking of each other as a person.
It is knowing that no matter where you go
or who you are, there is someone who truly loves you
and is always there to support and console you.
When a situation seems impossible, you make it through
together by holding on to each other.
It is strong enough to withstand harsh words and hurt
feelings, for it is smart enough to always see the
love beyond the words.
It is brave enough to always speak the truth, even
when lies would be easier.
It is always there — anytime, anywhere — whenever it
is needed.
It is a gift held in the heart and in the soul, and it
cannot be taken away or exchanged for another.
To possess this love is a treasure
that makes life more valuable.

— Stephanie Douglass

"I Love You, Mom"

Sons seem to have difficulty
    putting their feelings into words,
but that doesn't mean
    those feelings aren't there.
So many times I look at my mother
    and feel such affection and love,
yet I say nothing.
I have wonderful memories of times
    we shared that
she might think I don't remember —
    but I do.
Growing up as her son was fun,
    happy, and good.
Being the mother that she is,
I wouldn't be surprised if
    she already knows how I feel...
I love her very much!

— R. Hannan

"I Love You, Son"

Beyond words that can even begin
to tell him how much,
I hold him and his happiness
within my heart each and every day.

I am so proud of him and so thankful
to the years that have given me
so much to be thankful for.

If I were given a chance to be
anything I wanted to become,
there's nothing I would rather be
...than his mother.

And there is no one
I would rather have
...as my son.

— Laurel Atherton

It's a Boy!

"It's a boy," she said. "You have a boy."

You appeared before me, so secure in the support of our doctor's lean hand that it was quite invisible.... It was the movement of your lips that most impressed me. They curved in a small bow. You seemed to turn your head — although it must have merely bobbed away from the finger bracing it — and as it moved your lips curled upward in discovery, suddenly aware of the feel of some new element. Your tongue made a smack inside, and your lips parted and admitted your first breath of life. You sucked the air inside, and released it with a vocal sound....

I knew none of the people there, except our doctor, and yet I could see that behind their masks everyone was smiling. I realized then that everyone smiles at a birth. The species rejoices in itself.

Everyone smiles. And yet, no one really knows the rapture in the mother but herself. It is hers alone, never quite to be imagined by others, even by her child, unless perhaps on the day his own is born. I marvel at it. I felt united by a total, physical wonder. It must then be a thing outside any human explaining, at one with the miracle of birth itself.

— Charlotte Painter

What Is a Son?

A son is a warm spot in your heart and a smile on your lips.

In the beginning, he is charmingly innocent, putting his complete trust in you.

He comes to you for a hand to hold, and for the security only your arms can provide.

He shares his tales of adventure and knows how proud you are of his discoveries and accomplishments.

All his problems can be solved by a hug and a kiss from you, and the bond you share is so strong it is almost tangible.

Times passes, and your innocent little boy starts to test his limits. He lets go of your hand to race into the midst of life without thinking ahead or looking both ways.

His problems have grown along with him, and he has learned that you can't always make his life better or kiss his troubles away.

He spends much of his time away from you, and though you long for the closeness you once shared, he chooses independence and privacy.

Discoveries and accomplishments aren't as easy to come by now, and sometimes he wonders about his worth.

But you know the worth of that young man. He is your past and your future. He is hopes and dreams that have made it through each and every disappointment and failure.

In your heart, your son is precious and treasured. Together, you struggled through the years trying to find the right amount of independence for each new stage of his life, until finally, you had to learn to let him go.

Now you put your trust in him, leaving that son whom you hold so dear totally in his own care. You hope he always remembers that you have a hand for him to hold and arms to provide comfort or support.

Most of all, you hope that he believes in himself as much as you believe in him, and that he knows how much you love him.

— Barbara Cage

No Greater Joy

———————➤———————

*L*ike most women, I thought I wanted
at least one daughter, but after giving
birth to two sons, I have never grieved
not having had a female child.... I have
always felt that my sons were placed in
my custody to teach me something: if
you want to learn what makes a man,
watch a boy grow up.

— Patricia Stevens

I remember when he was so tiny that I could
cradle him in my arms and watch him sleep —
so oblivious to the world. When he awoke, he'd
smile at me and curl all his fingers around one
of mine, and hold on so very tightly that
I thought he'd never let go.

Those same precious fingers wound themselves
around my heart, too... and to this day, they
have never let go.

— Maria Shockley Erman

"Mama's Boys"

The life of every single man begins
not singly but with his mother. Baseball
coaches and businessmen, artists and
architects: we all were, at one time, mama's
boys. Every analyst who watches a
computer screen, and every farmer who
watches the weather used to watch his
mother's face the whole day long.
Regardless of where or how we eventually
grow up, our first years revolve around one
woman, and she is our ticket back to them.

— Nicholas Weinstock

The god to whom little boys say their prayers
has a face very much like their mother's.

— Sir James M. Barrie

$\mathcal{M}$y mother welcomed me into the world
and made sure I had everything I needed.
Through her constant presence
    and careful guidance,
she taught me the meaning of safety
    and security.

I used these twin foundations to find my way
    through the maze of childhood
and all the choices and challenges of life.
Along the way, her confidence in me
    and her acceptance of my mistakes
taught me what it means to have faith
    in myself.

We've shared birthdays, holidays,
and a million everyday moments
that still shine in my memories.
By always taking time to keep us
    all close,
she taught me the meaning of family.

I realize now that all along,
    in everything she did and said,
she was actually teaching me
    the meaning of love.
And my heart in return
    will love her forever.

— Edmund O'Neill

It Wasn't Always Easy

There were moments when all I wanted
to do was hold him in my arms and tell him
everything would be all right. But as a parent,
sometimes my job was more than just giving
a reassuring hug. I had to let him find out
things for himself, even when the outcome
was painful. It wasn't always easy, but I
believed it was necessary.

If I allowed him to think that any problem he
ever had would go away just by wishful
thinking, I wouldn't have been fulfilling my role
as a parent. He had to learn and grow
through his own trials and experiences —
slowly but surely building self-confidence
and courage with every step he took.

I encouraged him to be himself, feel
comfortable with who he is, and not let any
obstacle in front of him frighten him away.
I tried to teach him courage and positive
thinking to guide him over uncertain waters.

I did the best I could with whatever tools
I had. I wasn't a perfect parent, but I tried.
And through all the tears and the worrying,
he turned out just fine.

— T. L. Nash

The Challenges and the Rewards

After my son was born, my life became a challenge. Seeing his poised big sister, who did everything right, he escaped out of his crib, knocked over the houseplants, and decorated a closet wall with a bright blue marker.

He didn't hesitate to scare me. When I was eight months pregnant and waddling around like a beached whale, he fell in the bathtub. I had to take him to get stitches, and as the doctor sewed his chin, he told jokes and laughed and named the stitches "my itches."

I can still see him as he was back then... those bright eyes, his excitement over a frog, picking green tomatoes, covered in birthday cake, drinking pool water, climbing a pecan tree, kissing a neighbor's puppy, and running naked down the cul-de-sac.

From him, I learned the art of patience, the joy of mothering a son, and that there are never enough hours for cuddling and reading. Although he was so young, he taught me well, and I will always hold in my heart my gratitude for my son.

— Alice J. Wisler

The challenge for mothers of sons is to realize that because we do not share a sexual identity, that because we have not grown up in a male body, we cannot presume to understand everything there is to know about our sons' world. There is as much to learn from the experience of raising young men as there is to teach young men about what it is to be female.

— Patricia Stevens

From a baby, to a boy, to a young man, he was full of life and filled with surprises. Trying to keep up with him has been many things: rewarding, challenging, hopeful, and fulfilling. In every one of his years, he has given me more happiness and love than most people will ever even dream of.

— Marin McKay

The love of mother is never exhausted.

— Maurice Maeterlinck

Boys Will Be Boys

Sons do not roam through life without boundaries. Laws are to be made and enforced, and a mother is usually the first one to do so. Bedtimes and mealtimes, morals and manners: she is there to lay them all out and to monitor her son's performance. Boys commonly gripe about being saddled with rules and regulations, yet perhaps that's because they need them. We are boisterous and brash… and functioning at the mercy — and at the vanguard — of a worldwide trend of young male rowdiness. In fact, it's boyish yanking against mothers' limits that creates the fun and flirtation that sons enjoy with the woman in charge. We stick pencils up our noses, punch our brothers, pinch our sisters, and sprint around the house when it's time for our baths, laughing wildly until our mothers can't help but join us. In other words, sons can't lose. If we play by the rules, then we're golden; if we break them, well, then boys will be boys.

— Nicholas Weinstock

Growing and Learning Together

When my son came into this world and into my life, so many beautiful things happened. Although I was the one holding him, he was the one enfolding so many of my hopes and dreams. Although I was the one who was supposed to teach him all the things to do as he grew up, he was the one who taught me — constantly — of my capacity to love, to experience life in its most meaningful way, and to open my heart wide enough to let all those joyful feelings inside.

— Laurel Atherton

In his face I sometimes see
Shadowings of the man to be,
And eager, dream of what my son
Will be in twenty years and one.
But when he is to manhood grown,
And all his manhood ways are known,
Then shall I, wistful, try to trace
The child he once was in his face?

— Julia Johnson Davis

*E*ven when they were thirteen and fifteen, before either of them had a license to drive, I felt in many ways protected by these budding young men, who by then had already begun to tower over me. They taught me to be more adventurous *(Let's see where this unpaved road leads us)*, to face fear head-on *(Bears are as afraid of people as people are of them)*, to be less uptight when things don't go as planned *(So what if we've forgotten the tarp that goes over the tent roof and the rain is coming in through the net ceiling)*. They taught me to respect and admire differences, showed me that I can marvel at the intensity of their interest in fly-fishing or rebuilding car engines when I have no inclination to take up either of those myself.

— Patricia Stevens

*T*he outrages of adolescence pass. But its excitement can linger to flavor the future relationship of mother and son. It is the excitement of seeing a boy become a man, a man you never imagined, a man bursting forth from the child you love. It is the excitement of the unknown, of having no idea what manner of boy or beast (or so it sometimes seems) will be with you this day. It is the excitement of forming a new relationship, a more equal relationship, with the man who stands in place of the boy. It is the good sheer fun of watching your son grow up. For women who refuse to just sit back and wither with the years, it is the exhilarating joy of growing along with him.

— Joan Solomon Weiss

I Hope He'll Remember...

I hope he'll remember the times we spent together reading stories, playing games, exploring new places. I hope he'll remember the times we took walks together, talked, and laughed about things that happened to us. I hope he'll remember when we worked together as a team — I helped him and he helped me; we worked hard, we got dusty and dirty, but we had an awesome bond.

I hope he'll remember my arms around him, my kiss on his cheek, my hugs holding him as close as my heart. I hope he'll remember my pats on his back and my words of encouragement and comfort. I hope he'll remember my tucking him in at night and trying to keep his room monster-proof.

I hope he'll remember the times I *didn't* embarrass him when he was a teen and my pride when he got his driver's license, his first real-world job, and his first apartment.

I hope he'll remember...

— Jacqueline Schiff

An Unspoken Journey

A son is struck not only by the potency of a mother's support but by the direction it nudges him: away, most often, from her. The lofty dreams she puts in our heads cannot be played out in her living room. The home life she gathers and bolsters is geared to help us thrust ourselves great lengths from that home. Boys realize this and recover quickly, leading their own charges into their own futures. But their starts in life are often stuttering and ambivalent, regardless of how they may appear. Sooner or later, a son accepts and even embraces his role as boundless adventurer, as well as a mother's role as the one who watches him go. But for him to get to that point requires an arduous and unspoken journey.

— Nicholas Weinstock

*A*s he grew up, it was always my goal to be there if he needed me, and at the same time teach him responsibility for his own life. That is not an easy task, and I know I have failed at times. But I always did the best I could. I could not be more proud than I am now of the person he has become: a man full of understanding, respect for his fellow man, and sensitivity; a man on his way to becoming a success.

— Lynda Channing-Weber

*N*obody knows what a boy is worth, and the world must wait and see; for every man in an honored place, is a boy that used to be.

— Author Unknown

A Mother's Advice to Her Son

Carry On

Carry on as I would, Son.
Lay your problems down to rest.
Put all bad times behind you
and strive to be your best.

Carry on with confidence;
your hands now hold the reins.
Don't think your talents won't compare,
for my blood runs through your veins.

Carry on with honesty;
you know what's right and fair.
Just call on me when problems strike;
you know that I'll be there.

Carry on the dream, my son.
Let your conscience be your guide.
Remember when you feel alone,
I'm standing by your side.

— Shelley McDaniel

The Greatest Success of All

My son, if you give
   a part of yourself to life,
the part you receive back
   will be so much greater.
Never regret the past,
   but learn by it.
Never lose sight of your dreams;
a person who can dream
   will always have hope.
Believe in yourself;
   if you do, everyone else will.
You have the ability
   to accomplish anything,
   but never do it at
      someone else's expense.
If you can go through life loving others,
   you will have achieved
      the greatest success of all.

— Judy LeSage

Famous Sons Writing About Their Mothers

⟶

My mother was the making of me. She was so true and so sure of me. I felt that I had someone to live for — someone I must not disappoint. The memory of my mother will always be a blessing to me.

— Thomas A. Edison

My ever-loved Mother, I salute you with my affection once more, and thank you for bringing me into this world, and for all your unwearied care over me there. May God reward you for it, as assuredly He will and does.

— Thomas Carlyle

My mother made a brilliant impression upon my childhood life. She shone for me like the evening star — I loved her dearly.

— Winston Churchill

My mother was an angel on earth.

— John Quincy Adams

My mother had a great deal of
trouble with me but I think she enjoyed it.

— Samuel Clemens (Mark Twain)

I occupy myself... still enveloped in thoughts
of my dear mother, the most perfect and
magnetic character, the rarest combination of
practical, moral and spiritual, and the least
selfish, of all and any I have ever known —
and by me O so much the most deeply loved.

— Walt Whitman

And for you, dear Mummy, you know that
nothing can ever change what we have
always been and always will be to each other.

— Franklin Delano Roosevelt

All that I am or hope to be,
I owe to my sainted mother.

— Abraham Lincoln

A Mother's Love Is Forever

*W*ithin the shelter of a mother's wings, a son finds reassurance and encouragement and a precious kind of love. In the sound of her voice, he hears guidance, understanding, and so much hope.

Every time he thinks of the smiles in her eyes, he is reminded of a happiness that is very essential to the family ties they share. In the bond that always lives on in their hearts, he has come to know how much he's always counted on her.

There are so many days when he wishes he could find a way... to sincerely and dearly thank her. She brought him into the world and did everything she could to make it his very own heaven on earth. She has always done her very best to give him a feeling of self-worth and inner beauty. Even in the times when he may have caused her concern, she never gave up on him. He always felt her there; he always knew he was in her prayers and in her heart's warmest wishes.

To this very day, there is no one who gives such a sweetness to everything; no one anywhere who gives so much and asks so little in return; no one so much
　　　　　like an angel should be
　　　　　than a mother.

— Ceal Carson

Always There for Each Other

No matter what the son's age, Mother will always be an important and necessary home base for him: still setting limits and boundaries; still available for talks, problem solving, political discussions, and advice about love; still nurturing and understanding when life gets hard.

— Jeanne and Don Elium

Though time has lessened
his reliance on me,
prompting him to be more dependent
on his own good instincts in life,
I'm always here for him.
I'll always care as much as ever —
even more as the years go by —
for a mother's love and concern
continue on and grow throughout time,
oblivious to age, independence,
or any other condition,
except for the bond of love.
He'll always be my son,
and I'll always be his mother.

— Barbara J. Hall

$\mathcal{R}$eal men protect their mothers. For every kid old enough to make a fist, it's an instinctive and powerful reaction. For sons who have grown older, it's a gratifying method of looking out for their mothers and achieving their male status at once. The toughest, shiest, and most nonchalant among us rages against any danger to his mother. Just as a mother's impulse is to protect her baby, that baby grows to feel like her protector in return.

— Nicholas Weinstock

$\mathcal{T}$here could never have been in my mother's mind any conflict between her children's happiness and her own; they were to her one and the same thing.

— Harrison Rhodes

To My Son, with Love

A mother tries to provide her son
with insight into the important things in life
in order to make his life
as happy and fulfilling as possible

A mother tries to teach her son
to be kind and generous towards other people
to be honest and forthright at all times
to be fair, treating men and women equally
to respect and learn from older people
to know himself well
to understand his strong and weak points
to accept criticism and learn from his mistakes
to have many interests to pursue
to have many goals to follow
to work hard to reach these goals

A mother tries to teach her son
to have a strong set of beliefs
to listen to his intelligence
to laugh and enjoy life
to appreciate the beauty of nature
to express his feelings openly
    and honestly at all times
to realize that love is the best emotion
    that anyone can have
to value the family unit
    as the basis of stability

If I have provided you with an insight
into most of these things
then I have succeeded as a mother
in what I hoped to accomplish in raising you
If many of these things slipped by
while we were all so busy
I have a feeling that you know them anyway
And as your proud mother
I will always continue to love and support
everything you are and everything you do
I am always here for you, my son
I love you

— Susan Polis Schutz

A Loving Tribute to My Mother...

So many years have passed between us
since the first time you held me
and told me you would always love me.
So many memories have brought us
    close together over the years.
There was a time in my life when you
pulled me as close as you could
    to your heart,
because you felt I needed you.
Thank you — I did.
There were times in my life when
I needed your strength to walk
and your vision to see.
Thank you for being there for me.
However, your honesty is the most
valuable quality I have gained
    from you over the years.
It has helped me to see who I am,
and it helps me enable others
    to accept themselves. Thank you.
There are many other wonderful qualities
you have given me through your love,
and I hope I have said "thank you"
    for them along the way.

Every day, I think about how fortunate
I am to have a mother as special as you
    in my life.
If I could ever choose to start my life
    over again,
I wouldn't change a thing —
except the number of times I've told
    you "I love you,"
for that can't be expressed enough.
I hope that I have been the son
    you always wanted,
because you are the mother
I will always love.

— Antony Simpson

A Mother and Her Son

With patience and love
she guided him,
kissed away his hurts,
and hugged away loneliness.
She struggled to give him birth,
then struggled to give him
the independence he craved.
But the most difficult
thing she did of all
was to stand back and let him
learn his own lessons.

She worried each time he left home
or faced a new situation alone.
She guarded his heart and his life
the best she could,
and saw in him hopes and dreams
of the future.
She knew he could be anything
he wanted to be;
all he needed was to use
the drive and determination
within himself.

And as it should be,
the baby grew into a man,
and she was filled with a mixture
of sadness and pride:
    sadness, for days gone by;
    and pride, for with his help,
    she had done a good job
    of raising him.

— Barbara Cage

From 6 Years to Full Grown...
in the Blink of an Eye

An angel living near the moon
Walked through the sky and sang a tune
Plucking stars to make his crown —
And suddenly two stars fell down,
Two falling arrows made of light.
Six years ago this very night
I saw them fall and wondered why
The angel dropped them from the sky —
But when I saw your eyes I knew
The angel sent the stars to you.

— Sara Teasdale

I remember his years of growing,
all our shared thoughts and feelings,
the carefree and happy times a family shares.
I remember the joy, the tears, and the sorrow —
stormy emotions for changing times.
I remember the squeeze of his hand,
whispered "I love you's,"
the snapshots and memories of time and years.
I remember all the ways he's made my heart proud.

— Linda E. Knight

A Mother Sees Her Son

My greatest gift
   has been to see the person
   that my son has become —
To see his strength,
   to share his laughter,
   to watch with delight
   as he becomes
An individual who adds
   joy to the world.

Thinking back,
I see reflections of his childhood —
   fragments of laughter and tears,
   courage and disappointments.
But mostly, I see images
   of his smile, his perseverance,
   and his love
And I look on in wonder
   at the person he has become.

I hope he will always treasure
   our times together
   and add them to the tapestry
   of his life —
Weaving those memories
   of love and laughter
Together with the joy
   that comes from being
   in the presence of unending love —
The kind that comes
   from a mother's heart to her son.

— Norma Noraker McGihon

A Son's Thank-You

If there is happiness in my heart,
    it's because my mother helped put it there.
If there is gentleness in my beliefs,
    it's because she showed me how to care.
If there is understanding in my thinking,
    it's because she shared her wisdom.

If there is a rainbow over my shoulder,
    it's because of her outlook and her vision.
If there is a knowledge that I can reach out —
    and I really can make some dreams come true —
    it's because I learned from the best
    teacher of all... my mother.

                        — Chris Gallatin

A Mother's Wishes

That my son will be filled with an awareness
    of who he is and where he is going;
that he will find happiness
    with people he loves and who love him;
that he will always be open to
    new possibilities of learning;
that he will never give up his dreams;
that he will be a caring, thoughtful person;
and most of all,
that he will remember that his mother loves him
and will always be there for him
    throughout his life.

                    — Jesse Rose Thompson

Learning to Let Go

My son's slippers rest on a wool hooked rug by the side of his bed. They have sat there for a week, untouched, like everything else in his room. I try not to go in there much; the sense of emptiness I feel, of something missing, grieves me.... I force myself to imagine him having a wonderful time at sleepaway camp, but his letters don't reveal anything. *Dear Mom and Dad,* he writes, *They make us write a letter before we can have lunch. I'm hungry. Love, Reid (your son).*

I wanted him to take his slippers, but he was adamantly particular about footwear. He wore his favorite sneakers and brought along only a pair of blue mesh water shoes, despite my exaggerated warnings about frosty Adirondack mornings and potential mud slides. In a convincing, rather macho display, he insisted he would make do.

I thought of him mornings at camp, gingerly walking barefoot across the cold, splintery plywood floor. Telling myself he'd be glad in the end, I'd considered packing his slippers at the last moment, tucking them into his canvas duffel, where he might find them while he was putting away his things. I had wrapped the slippers in a plastic bag, was about to slide them in, when I was overcome by a strong and remarkably discomfiting feeling. Betrayal.

As I unwrapped the slippers and carefully place them on his rug, I thought, they're his feet, after all. And step by step, they will take him away from me.

— Valerie Monroe

I have loved
watching him go through life
as only a child can...
    laughing, crying,
      so sure of himself,
and at the same time
      so often full of doubts.
My heart broke for him
      when life was unfair;
I would have shielded him
from pain and heartache
      if he had let me.
I wanted to protect him,
but he needed to grow
into his own person,
so I had to let go —
a little at a time.
That was one of the hardest
things I've ever had to do.

His childhood is gone now,
    and I still miss those
      wonderful times,
but I am so proud of
the adult he has become.
Whatever paths in life
he may choose to embrace,
    my love will be with him...
and I will cherish him always.

— Peggy Selig

On Having a Grown-Up Son

As a child, he was full of
laughter and hugs,
challenges and successes,
contentment and pride —
and that really hasn't
changed much
as he's grown into a man.

To say that I love him
seems small and insignificant
compared to the deep feelings
    I have for him.
I feel so much more
        than words can express.
His voice still makes me stop
and reflect on how fortunate I am
        to have him.
His smile and his laughter
        still cheer me
and bring me happiness.
His success, attitude, and actions
have a direct influence on my own.

And though there were times
when I've tried to distance myself
to give him the freedom and space
he needed and craved,
I was never able to.
No matter where he is
or what he is doing,
he is my son —
and that makes him a unique
and highly important individual
who means everything to me.

— Barbara Cage

When a Son Becomes a Father

I saw my tough, cool, macho son
fall in love with a baby this week.

I saw my somewhat arrogant son
come apart when the baby cried this week.

I saw my son melt with tenderness
when he watched the baby nursing this week.

I saw my son overcome with joy
when the baby smiled in his sleep this week.

I saw my rather fastidious son
change a diaper this week.

I saw my son
become a father this week.

— Natasha Josefowitz

I remember when he was born;
   I experienced a feeling beyond words.
Now he has children of his own
   and knows that feeling, too.

I remember teaching him how to
   do things for the first time.
Now the roles have changed,
   and he has become the teacher.

I remember losing sleep on nights
   when he had a fevered brow.
Now he walks the floor
   when his children become ill.

I remember making sacrifices
   so he could have a little more.
Now I see him making
   the same sacrifices for his children.

I remember the pride I felt
   when he wanted his friends to meet me.
Now I see him standing tall when
   his children want to show him off.

My grandchildren are blessed
   to have a father like my son,
just as having him for a son
   has brought joy to my life.

— Karen Richey

What It's like to Raise a Son

To be completely honest, raising a son can sometimes be difficult for a mother. There are the obvious differences between the two, as well as other things that many women just can't understand from the male point of view.

There are times when a boy needs to test his strength, while his mother worries that he will get hurt. There are times when male pride prevents a son from discussing things with his mother, even when she thinks it will make him feel better. There are times when a mother is simply "wrong" because she "doesn't understand."

Somehow, my son and I made it through these times. Somewhere along the way, we gained respect for each other's opinions, even if we didn't always understand them. There is no one else I would rather have shared all of our experiences with, both good and bad.

— Vicki Perkins

Where Did the Time Go?

When I look at my son now,
I see a man standing there,
and I wonder how this could be.
It was only a short time ago
that I held him in my arms
and rocked his tears away.
Just last week,
I wiped his runny nose
and bragged about how
he could ride a bike.
Only yesterday,
I attended his graduation.
I noticed then that I had
to stretch up to kiss him.

He is a man now, proud and wise,
strong in body and spirit.
I don't know how
he accomplished this so quickly;
I only know that he is
as important to me now
as he was at all those times past.
I still brag about his achievements
with the same pride,
and I'd help heal his hurts
if he needed me to.
I know he doesn't need me the way
that he used to, and
I share his joy for his independence.
The years slip away,
but my love for him remains
as strong as when I first held him.

— Fran Knutson

Coming Full Circle

There once was a time,
a long time ago it seems,
when I held his hand to
cross the street; now he holds mine.
There once was a time,
a long time ago it seems,
when he rested his head in my arms;
now it is the gentle strength
of his shoulders
that comforts me.

Life goes full circle,
and the young and the old
walk together through time.
I am so proud because once upon a time,
a long time ago it seems,
a baby boy was born
who now is a man...
    following his dreams.

— Dena Dilaconi

The Best Mother

Somehow, my mother always managed
to make me feel I could do anything.
She said it and showed it
in so very many ways.
Even today, as an adult, I know
she believes in me
and always thinks the best of me.
Maybe I could repay her
for all the money she's spent on me,
but I can never repay her for the time,
words of encouragement, guidance,
support, and love
she's given me over the years.
Being a mother is a lifelong achievement.
To me, my mother is the best mother
I could have hoped for.

— John Ray

A Most Wonderful Son

My son has been such a wonderful
   gift to my life.
The pride and happiness
   he has given me
cannot compare with anything else.
The smiles, the fun, and laughter
   we've shared,
are countless and precious.
Memories of him fill my heart
   and my mind,
and anytime I am down or lonely,
all I have to do is recall them.
There is nothing more fulfilling
   or rewarding
than parenting a son.

— Barbara Cage

Mothers and Sons Share an Unbreakable Bond of Love and Appreciation

The love between mother and son needs few words, but is the foundation for all we give by being there, by sharing time and effort, by our talks, and by our caring.

— Ruthann Tholen

Our relationship
may seem to have changed
over the years,
but I know our love hasn't.
The bond we share can't be changed;
we are together even when we are apart,
for we are forever in each other's heart.

— Barbara Cage

ACKNOWLEDGMENTS

We gratefully acknowledge the permission granted by the following authors, publishers, and authors' representatives to reprint poems or excerpts from their publications.

Charlotte Painter for "It's a boy..." from WHO MADE THE LAMB, published by McGraw-Hill Book Co. Copyright © 1988 by Charlotte Painter. All rights reserved.

Brandt and Hochman Literary Agents, Inc., for "Like most women, I thought...," "The challenge for mothers of sons...," and "Even when they were thirteen..." by Patricia Stevens and "My son's slippers..." by Valerie Monroe from BETWEEN MOTHERS AND SONS, edited by Patricia Stevens, published by Scribner. Copyright © 1999 by Patricia Stevens. All rights reserved.

Riverhead Books, a division of Penguin Putnam, Inc., and Watkins/Loomis Agency for "The life of every single man...," "Sons do not roam through life...," "A son is struck not only...," and "Real men protect..." from THE SECRET LIVES OF SONS by Nicholas Weinstock. Copyright © 1997 by Nicholas Weinstock. All rights reserved.

Alice J. Wisler for "After my son was born...." Copyright © 2003 by Alice J. Wisler. All rights reserved.

Lowenstein-Morel Associates, Inc., for "The outrages of adolescence..." from RAISING A SON: THE ESSENTIAL GUIDE TO A HEALTHY MOTHER-SON RELATIONSHIP by Joan Solomon Weiss, published by Summit Books. Copyright © 1985 by Joan Solomon Weiss. All rights reserved.

Celestial Arts, a division of Ten Speed Press, for "No matter what the son's age..." from RAISING A SON: PARENTS AND THE AWAKENING OF A HEALTHY MAN by Jeanne Elium and Don Elium. Copyright © 1994, 1996 by Jeanne Elium and Don Elium. All rights reserved.

Barbara Cage for "A Mother and Her Son." Copyright © 2003 by Barbara Cage. All rights reserved.

Natasha Josefowitz for "I saw my tough, cool, macho son..." from NATASHA'S WORDS FOR FAMILIES. Copyright © 1986 by Natasha Josefowitz. All rights reserved.

A careful effort has been made to trace the ownership of selections used in this anthology in order to obtain permission to reprint copyrighted material and give proper credit to the copyright owners. If any error or omission has occurred, it is completely inadvertent, and we would like to make corrections in future editions provided that written notification is made to the publisher:

BLUE MOUNTAIN ARTS, INC., P.O. Box 4549, Boulder, Colorado 80306.